A HISTORICAL TIMELINE OF WINE

ISBN-10:1519533144
ISBN-13:978-1519533142

DEDICATION

Field Of Master would like to dedicate this book to winemakers, who use their love of earth, fruit and life-learned talents in combination with God's rich goodness to share their art of wine with the world. Also to the wine enthusiast who appreciate and enjoy God's blessings in "the finer things of life."

ANCIENT BEGINNINGS

Wine making is thought to have originated in the area between the Black Sea, Caspian Sea, and the Sea of Galilee.

The Middle East and Eastern Mediterranean was the cradle of the world's wine culture thousands of years before the vine reached Europe.

The Biblical Book of Genesis first mentions the production of wine following the Great Flood. Noah was the first recorded viticulturist who, after the flood, "planted a vineyard."

7000 BC Jiahu – The first chemical trace of any fermented beverage. Jiahu, is located in China's Yellow River valley. This more than 9,000-year-old concoction was a mix of rice, honey and fruit.

7000 BC discoveries show that early winemaking used hollowed out logs filled with grapes. The grapes were treaded under foot and the juice and crushed grape remains were then scooped into jars to ferment.

5400 BC Hajji Firuz Tepe, West Azarbaijan province in northwestern Iran-ceramic jars were found to contain the residue of two chemicals: tartaric acid, which occurs in grapes and resin from an evergreen tree. Wine in the ancient world was often resonated. These jars have been recognized as the earliest conclusive chemical evidence of winemaking.

4500 BC Wine production spreads to Greater Iran and Grecian Macedonia.

4200 BC Docile Tash Greece – The earliest chemical evidence of wine in Europe discovered in the Eastern Macedonia region of Greece. The ceramic vases, which contain the residue of thousands of carbonized grape pips together with the skins, makes this the oldest chemically confirmed wine in Europe.

4100 BC The oldest-known winery was discovered in the "Areni-1" cave in Vetoes Dzor, Armenia. The site contained a wine press, fermentation vats, jars, cups, V. vinifera seeds and vines.

3200 BC Domesticated grapes were abundant in the Near East from the beginning of the early Bronze Age.

Tomb paintings excavated at Thebes showed ancient Egyptians used long bars hanging over the treading basins with straps that workers would hold onto while treading grapes in their wine presses.

3100 BC wine found in ceramic jars at Godin Tepe in the Zagros Mountains of northwestern Iran.

The Tomb Of King Scorpion I Egypt - jars encrusted with wine residue found, present early evidence of wine trading. The 300 jars in the tomb, which the king intended to take to the afterlife, were made from clay from Palestine, which implies that the wine itself was imported from vineyards hundreds of miles away.

3000 BC The first glass was produced in Northern Syria. Evidence is found for winemaking in Sumer and Egypt. The ancient Romans were particularly well-known for their glasswork, which was used both domestically and industrially. They developed the technique of glassblowing, which was used to make wine bottles. The term "glass" was first used by the Romans.

A thriving royal winemaking industry was established in the Nile Delta following the introduction of grape cultivation from the Levant to Egypt. The industry was most likely started as the result of trade between Egypt and Canaan during the early Bronze Age, commencing from at least the 27th-century BC Third Dynasty, the beginning of the Old Kingdom period.

Wine in ancient Egypt was predominantly red. Due to its resemblance to blood, much superstition surrounded wine-drinking in Egyptian culture.

1730 BC Glasswork was found to have been used in South Asia.

1700 BC Archaeologists recently discovered an approximately 3700 year old wine cellar in northern Israel. More than 500 gallons of wine were once stored in this cellar, enough to fill 3,000 bottles.

1600 BC One of the earliest known Greek wine presses was discovered in Palekastro in Crete and dated to the Mycenaean period. It was a stone basin for treading the grapes by feet with a run off drain for the juice to flow.

1550 BC Hieroglyphs and paintings show Egyptians using a type of cloth "sack press" where grapes or skins left over from treading would be twisted and squeezed by a tourniquet to release the juice.

1300 BC Tutankhamun's tomb - Residue discovered from five clay amphoras is white wine, revealing that white wine was available to the Egyptians through trade if not produced domestically. The 26 labeled jars of wine discovered in the tomb of King Tutankhamun include examples such as: "Year Four Wine of very good quality of the House-of-Aton of the Western River. Chief vintner Khay.

The use of a wine press in winemaking is mentioned frequently in the Bible. These presses were more elaboration of treading lagars where grapes that were tread by feet with the juice running off into special basins.

429 BC Pericles' Wine Cup – Greece. Pericles was an influential politician, orator, and general during Athens' Golden Age, which is also sometimes referred to as The Age Of Pericles. Pericles' wine cup was found, shattered into a dozen pieces, in the grave of a pauper, in a northern suburb of Athens, on Sparta Street.

Phoenicians were instrumental in distributing wine, wine grapes, and winemaking technology throughout the Mediterranean region through their extensive trade network. Phoenician-distributed grape varieties were important in the development of the wine industries of Rome and Greece.

Much of modern wine culture derives from the practices of the ancient Greeks. Many of the grapes grown in modern Greece are grown there exclusively and are similar or identical to the varieties grown in ancient times.

350 BC Lemnian wine, which is believed to be the same as the modern-day Lemnió varietal, a red wine with a bouquet of oregano and thyme. In his writings, Aristotle described a wine from the island of Lemos that was made from a grape, Limnia, that today is widely believed to be Limnio', the oldest known varietal still in cultivation

Greek wine was widely known and exported throughout the Mediterranean. The Greeks introduced the V. vinifera vine to and made wine in their numerous colonies in modern-day Italy, Sicily, southern France, and Spain.

2nd Century BC China-Archaeologists have discovered production from native "mountain grapes" like V. thunbergii and V. filifolia.

Winemaking equipment used to extract the juice from the skins is thought to have emerged during the Greco-Roman periods where written accounts by Cato the Elder, Marcus Terentius Varro, Pliny the Elder and others described wooden wine presses that utilized large beams, capstans and windlasses to exert pressure on the pomace. The wines produced by these presses were usually darker, with more color extracted from the skins but could also be more harsh with bitter tannins also extracted.

Zhang Qian's exploration of modern Xinjiang reached the Hellenistic successor states of Alexander's empire: Dayuan, Bactria, and the Indo-Greek Kingdom. These kingdom's had brought viticulture into Central Asia and trade permitted the first wine produced from V. vinifera grapes to be introduced to China.

Barrels were invented by the Gauls. The earliest known coopers tools date only from 100 BC but the art of barrel making is assumed to be much older.

1st Century AD - Winepress trough from the Old City of Jerusalem.

25 AD Jesus turns water into wine.

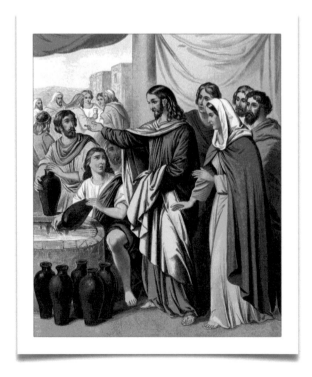

Later, Jesus incorporated the fruit of the vine as part of the Eucharist.

Wine is the most common alcoholic beverage mentioned in The Bible where it is a source of symbolism, and was an important part of daily life in biblical times.

The inhabitants of ancient Israel drank beer, and wines made from fruits other than grapes.

23 AD The writer Strabo wrote that the Gauls bought wine from northern Italy and then stored it in wooden containers that could be as large as a house. This observation has actually been supported by the discovery of remnants of wooden containers having capacities of over 1000 liters.

During the period of the Second Israelite Temple, winemaking was at its peak. It was a major export and economic mainstay. However, upon the destruction of the Second Temple and the dispersion of the Jews, the wine industry was forsaken in Israel.

79 A.D. Roman city of Pompeii. Mount Vesuvius erupted burying and preserving the city in ash and pumice. Pompeii was a major wine producer in Roman times. The city's fertile lands supported numerous wineries, which produced more than enough wine for the city. Wine from Pompeii was also exported up to Rome and other parts of the Empire. Pliny The Elder wrote about the wines:

"As to the wines of Pompeii, they have arrived at their full perfection in ten years, after which they gain nothing by age: they are found also to be productive of headache, which often lasts so long as [noon] of the next day."

79 AD Pliny the Elder, wrote that the Gauls stored their wine in wooden containers that were held together with metal hoops. He mentioned that storing wine in barrels made of yew made it poisonous. Pliny believed that the barrel was developed by Gallic tribes in the Alps and noted that it was used in colder countries, while elsewhere wine was stored in earthenware vases

AD 92 Emperor Domitian was forced to pass the first wine laws on record. Winemaking technology improved considerably during the time of the Roman Empire. During this time many grape varieties and cultivation techniques were developed. Viniculture expanded so much that wine laws were passed to ban the planting of new vineyards in Italy and to uproot half of the vineyards in the provinces. This was done to increase the production of the necessary but less profitable grain.

AD 600 The Arab conquest further weakened the wine industry, due to Islam's prohibition on alcohol. The wine industry in the Land of Israel lay dormant for another thousand years, until the return to Zion.

Wine was imported again when trade with the West was restored under the Tang dynasty. It remained mostly to the imperial royals and it was not until the Song that its consumption spread among the common people.

The Majority of the major wine-producing regions of Western Europe today were established during the Roman Imperial era.

Following the Greek invention of the screw wine presses became common in Roman villas.

The Romans created a precursor to today's appellation systems, as certain regions gained reputations for their fine wines.

The Roman upper class would dissolve pearls in wine for better health, as wine, mixed with herbs and minerals, was consumed to serve medicinal purpose.

325 - 350 AD The oldest surviving bottle still containing liquid wine, the Speyer wine bottle, belonged to a Roman nobleman.

5th Century - The Western Roman Empire falls. Europe enters a period of invasions and social turmoil, with the Roman Catholic Church as the only stable social structure. Through the Church, grape growing and winemaking technology, essential for the Mass, were preserved.

5th and 6th Centuries - In the Arabian peninsula before the advent of Islam, wine was traded by Aramaic merchants, as the climate was not well-suited to the growing of vines. Many other types of fermented drinks, were produced, including date and honey wines.

7th and 8th Centuries - The Muslim conquests brought many territories under Muslim control. Alcoholic drinks were prohibited by law, but the production of alcohol, wine in particular, thrived.

Christian monasteries in the Levant and Iraq cultivated grapevines and distributed their vintages in taverns located on monastery grounds.

Zoroastrians in Persia and Central Asia also engaged in the production of wine. They became known for their taverns that served their wines.

Wine in general found an industrial use in the Medieval Middle East as feedstock after advances in distillation by Muslim alchemists allowed for the production of relatively pure ethanol, which was used in the perfume industry. Wine was also for the first time distilled into brandy during this period.

1000 AD. Chateau de Goulaine in the Loire Valley was built. This is the oldest still operating winery in existence.

1100 A.D. Schloss Johannesburg in Germany is built.

In the Middle Ages, wine was the common drink of all social classes in the South, where grapes were cultivated. In the North and east, where few if any grapes were grown, beer and ale were the usual beverages. Wine was exported to the northern regions, but because of its relatively high expense was only consumed by the nobel class.

European appreciation of wine endured throughout the Middle Ages partly because drinking water was still unreliable, wine was the preferred alternative to accompany meals.

1200 AD First mention of Pinot Noir as Morillon.

Since wine was necessary, for the celebration of the Catholic Mass, assuring a supply was crucial. The Benedictine monks became one of the largest producers of wine in France and Germany, followed closely by the Cistercians.

A 13th-century Dominican, wrote a catalogue of all the known wines and ales of Europe.

The Benedictines owned vineyards in Champagne, Burgundy, and Bordeaux in France, and in the Rheingau and Franconia in Germany.

1304 First mention of Muscat Blanc as Muscatellus.

Viticulture and viniculture advanced thanks to the husbandry of Church monasteries across the continent, which gave rise to some of the finest vineyards in Europe.

1336 Cistercian Monks erect walled vineyard monastery called Clos de Vougeot in Burgundy Jofroi of Waterford.

1400 Wine is safer to drink than water.

1435 Count John IV of Katzenelnbogen, a wealthy member of the Holy Roman high nobility near Frankfurt, was the first to plant Riesling. The nearby winemaking monks made it into an industry, producing enough wine to ship all over Europe for secular use.

16th Century - The basket press became popular as winemaking technology advances were made by religious orders (particularly in France and Germany) who owned vast amounts of vineyard land and produced large quantities of wines in their abbeys and bishoprics. The press included large cylindrical basket made of wood staves bound together by wood or metal rings with a heavy horizontal disc fitted at the top. After the grapes were loaded into the basket, the disc would depress towards the bottom with juice seeping out between the staves into a waiting basin or tray.

Mexico becomes one of the most important wine producers. Its output begins to affect Spanish commercial production. In this competitive climate, the Spanish king sent an executive order to halt Mexico's production of wines and the planting of vineyards.

1500 Muscat, Pinot Noir, Tempranillo and Riesling are all common wines.

1530 Wine grapes are delivered to the New World by the Portuguese and Spanish in Mexico and Brazil.

In the 17th Century, the style of winemaking in France was for heartier wines that could age and survive long transport voyages over seas.

Madeira is vinho da roda- a wine that is improved by aging on sea voyages.

1650 Cabernet Sauvignon is born-a natural cross of Sauvignon Blanc and Cabernet Franc somewhere in Bordeaux.

1670 First vineyard planted at Chateau Lafite-Rothschild.

1680 Wine production began in the Cape Province of what is now South Africa.

1681 The earliest reference to a corkscrew. It was described as a "steel worm used for the drawing of corks out of bottles."

Bordeaux traded wine for coffee and other sought after items from the New World, helping to cement the role of wine in emerging world trade.

1693 Dom Pérignon monk and cellar master at the Benedictine abbey in Hautvillers, pioneered many winemaking techniques. He was thought to be the first to blend grapes to improve the quality of wines; perfected the art of producing clear white wines from black grapes; enhanced the tendency of Champagne wines to retain their natural sugar in order to naturally induce secondary fermentation; mastered deciding when to bottle wines in order to capture the bubble; introduced corks instead of wood, and used thicker glass in order to strengthen the bottles which were prone to explode at that time. He also achieved the grape mixes that now define Champagne.

European grape varieties were first brought to what is now Mexico by the first Spanish conquistadors to provide the necessities of the Catholic Holy Eucharist.

1752 Port wine is demarcated.

Popular wines include Madeira, Port, Sauternes and Sherry.

1775 The first late harvest 'noble rot' wines recorded at Schloss Johanisberg.

1788 Australia's First Fleet brought cuttings of vines from South Africa (although initial plantings failed and the first successful vineyards were established in the early 19th century).

With relatively modest changes, the basket press has continued to be widely used for centuries since its introduction by both small artisan winemakers to large Champagne houses. In Europe, basket presses with hydraulic machinery can be found throughout Sauternes, Burgundy and parts of Italy.

Nearly all prestigious Bordeaux wine estates were giving the grapes more time to ferment in the vat. They used a basket press for the darker vin vermeilh and pressed the wines into new oak barrels. Improved production techniques resulted in the emergence of finer qualities of wine, while glass bottles with corks began to be used.

1800 The era of Thomas Jefferson wine enthusiasm begins.

19th Century - The advancement of steam power machinery brought about a revolution in wine press technology as the manual basket press gave way to steam-powered presses. This greatly increased the efficiency of pressing and reduced the amount labor needed to operate a press.

The advancement of rail transport had a positive influence as the cost of transporting large wine presses from manufacturers to wine regions decreased. More wineries were able to afford purchasing a wine press.

1830 Modern bottle shape introduced.

1836 Wine to New Zealand.

1839 Settler George Calvert Yount built a homestead and was the first to plant grapes in Napa Valley.

The first recorded winery in Palenstine opened in 1848 by Rabbi Yitzhak Shor.

1857 Buena Vista - first commercial winery in California opens.

1861 Charles Krug is credited with establishing Napa Valley's first commercial winery.

1876 Beringer winery is established in Napa Valley

1879 Inglenook winery is established in Napa Valley by Gustave Niebaum.

1863 – The Great French Wine Blight

In the mid-19th century, Phylloxera aphids from North America appeared on vinis vitifera vines in the Languedoc region of France.

These aphids feed on leaves and roots, causing nodules and eventually killing the vine. Between the 1850s to mid-1870s, over 40% of French grape vines and vineyards were lost due to this infestation, and as a result the French economy suffered many lost businesses.

1870 During the devastating phylloxera blight in Europe, where 75% of France's vineyards were destroyed, native American vines were found to be immune to the pest. French-American hybrid grapes were developed and some were used in Europe.

1889 More than 40 wineries are in operation in Napa Valley.

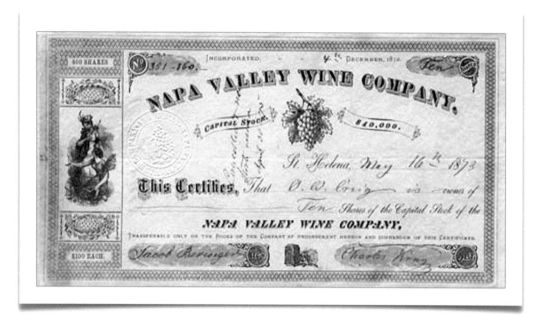

The practice of grafting European grapevines to American rootstocks was discovered to protect vineyards from the insect. Lessons learned from the infestation led to the positive transformation of Europe's wine industry. Bad vineyards were uprooted and their land turned to better uses. Some of France's best butter and cheese is now made from cows that graze on Charentais soil, which was previously covered with vines.

1870 Palestine winery was founded by Rabbi Avrom Teperberg. Efrat Winery was founded in the Old City in Jerusalem. The same year, the Mikveh Israel Agricultural School was founded southeast of Jaffa. Under French patronage, its wine school was the first to use European varietals.

1882 Baron Edmond de Rothschild commissioned a study to explore agricultural possibilities in Palestine and two years later, began producing grapes there. This was the beginning of the Carmel Winery.

"There are big wineries in Hungary, but not like this. I saw modern wineries in France, but not like this. What a great thing the Baron has done!" Theodore Herzl, following a visit in 1898.

1890 Zinfandel was the most popular grape in America.

In the 20th century, wine presses advanced from the vertical style to horizontal with pressure being applied at ends or sides through use of an airbag or bladder. These new presses had to have the pomace emptied and grapes reloaded. A belt or Archimedes' screw would subject the grapes to increasing pressure from one end of the press to the other. New grapes were continuously being added while the pomace was constantly being removed.

1900 Carmel No. 1 (Palestine) won the Gold Medal at the Paris Exhibition, along with some of the finest chateaux of Bordeaux.

Three future Israeli prime ministers:
David Ben Gurion in 1907, Levi Eshkol in 1915, and, decades later, Ehud Olmert, worked in Palestine's Carmel wineries and vineyards.

1920-1933 Prohibition.

1935 – Creation of the AOC Label & Institut National de l'origins et de la Qualité. The appellation d'origine controlee (AOC) was one of the first legal actions taken by the French to guarantee the origin and authenticity of an agricultural product in France, including wine.

1949 Bordeaux 'vintage of the century.'

Advancement in the horizontal batch press was the complete enclosure of the press, reducing the exposure of the grape must to air. Some advanced presses can even be flushed with nitrogen to create a complete anaerobic environment, desirable for wine making with white wine grapes.

1960's Israel sought advice from California and new planting of varietals such as Cabernet Sauvignon and Sauvignon Blanc were made.

1964 Sangria is introduced to United States.

1965 Box wine is invented by Thomas Angove a winemaker from Renmark, South Australia.

1976 Judgment of Paris and Wine Spectator's first issue. Until the latter half of the 20th century, American wine was generally viewed as inferior to that of Europe. However, with the surprisingly favorable American showing at the Paris Wine tasting of 1976, New World wine began to garner respect throughout the world.

Many of today's modern presses are computerized allowing the operator to control exactly how much pressure is being applied to the grape skins.

1978 - Robert Parker's establishes 100 Point Rating System
Prior to this rating system, wines were rated on a 20-point rating system which is still used today by several wine critics. This method was deemed "inflexible" by Parker, allowing for compressed ad inflated wine ratings. Basing his system on the 100-point American Standardized Grading system of the 1970s, he evaluated wines on a scale of 50-100, with wines rating 85 or higher considered "above average" or "good." These scores, published alongside tasting notes in The Wine Advocate, became wildly popular as a reference to determine drinkability and collectability.

1983 Phylloxera outbreak in Napa California.

1990 Israeli wine began winning international awards

2008 Robert Parker insures his nose for $1 million dollars.

2010 A bottle of 1869 Lafite-Rothschild sells for $230,000.

2016 1 Billion dollar 'Wine City' to open in Yantai, China.

ABOUT THE AUTHOR

Iris O'Brien is an Artist, Chef, Entrepreneur, Photographer, Writer, founder and owner of Field Of Masters.